AUDIO ACCESS INCLUDED
Recorded Backing Tracks Online

ONE VOICE

Praise AND Worship
SOLOS FOR TEENS
10 Songs with Instrumental Backing Tracks

Audio Arrangements by Larry Moore

To access companion recorded backing tracks online, visit:
www.halleonard.com/mylibrary

Enter Code
6210-2131-9937-6638

ISBN 978-1-4803-5227-8

HAL•LEONARD®
CORPORATION
7777 W. BLUEMOUND RD. P.O. BOX 13819 MILWAUKEE, WI 53213

Visit Hal Leonard Online at
www.halleonard.com

CONTENTS

Audio Arrangements by Larry Moore

Amazing Grace
(My Chains Are Gone)

Words by JOHN NEWTON
Traditional American Melody
Additional Words and Music by CHRIS TOMLIN
and LOUIE GIGLIO

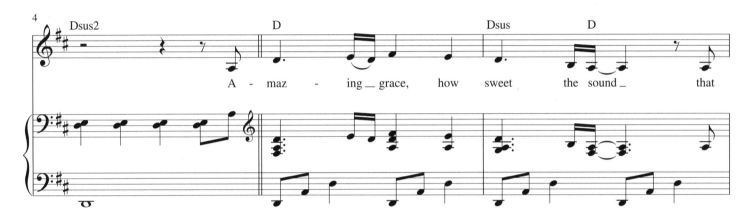

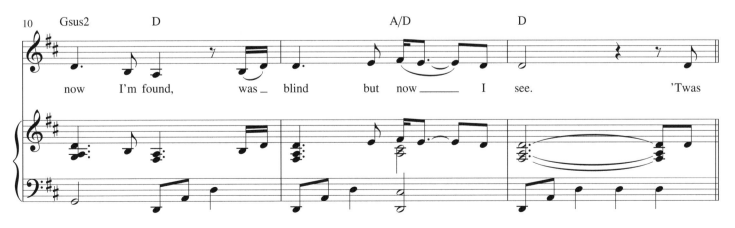

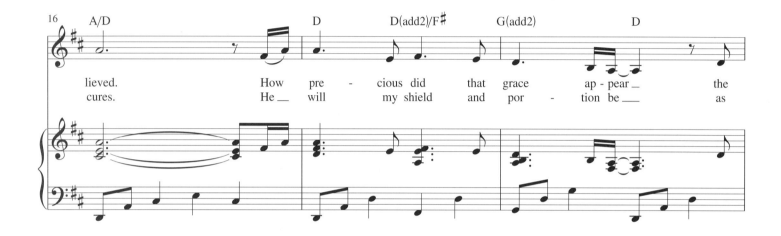

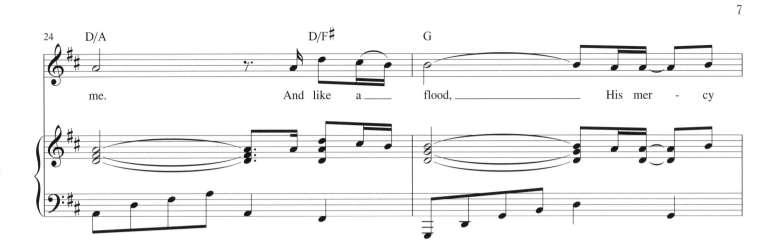

And like a ____ flood, _____ His mer - cy

rains un-end - ing love, a-maz - ing grace.

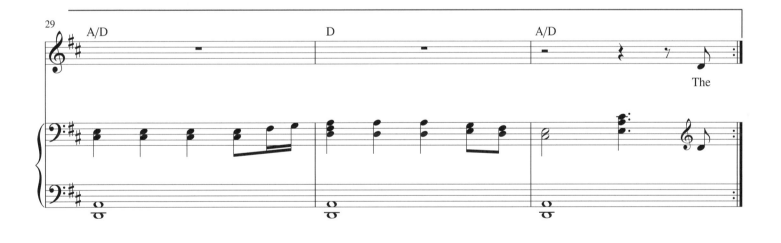

The

grace. My chains are gone, I've been set __ free. My God, my

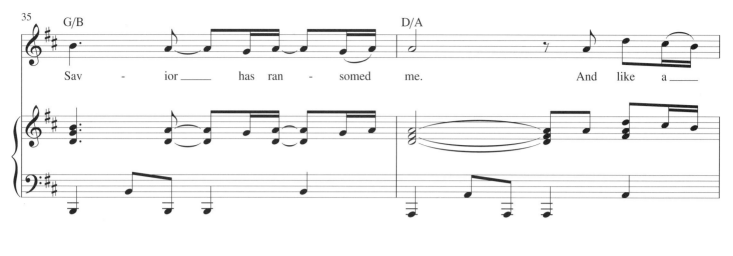

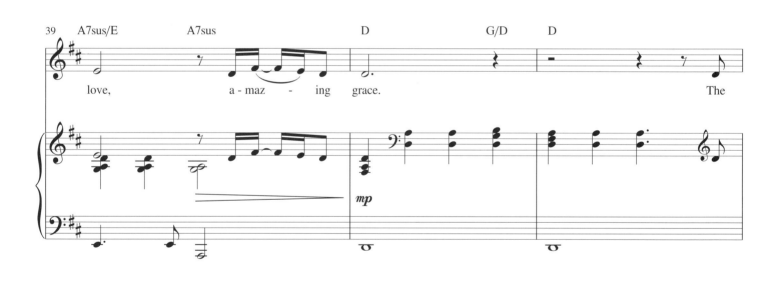

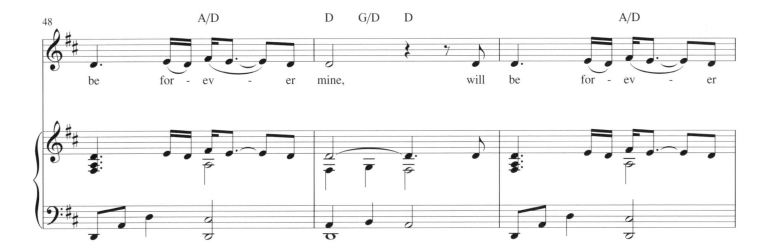

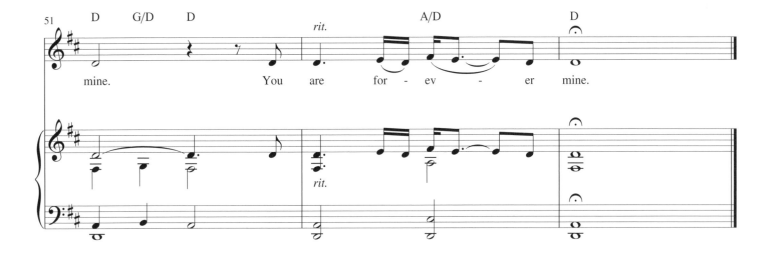

Hosanna

Words and Music by
BROOKE FRASER

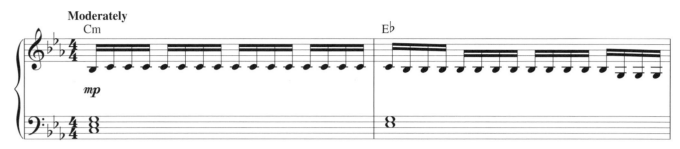

I see the King of ___ Glo - ry
I see a gen - er - a - tion

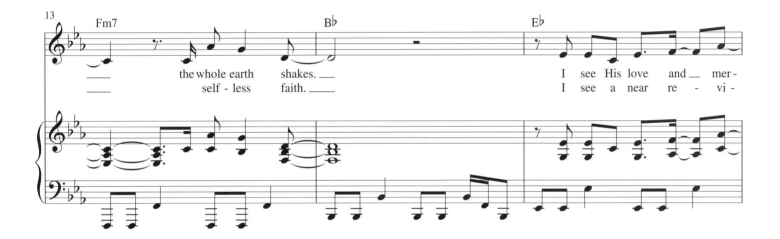

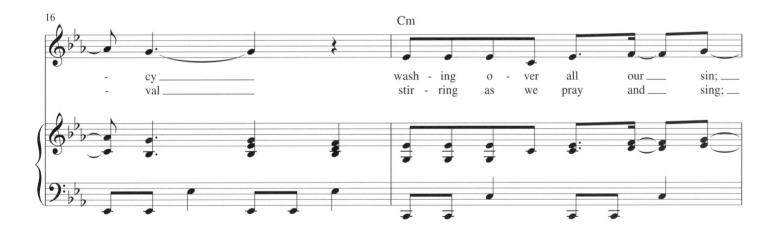

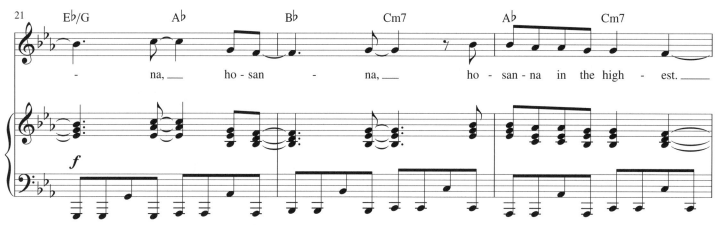

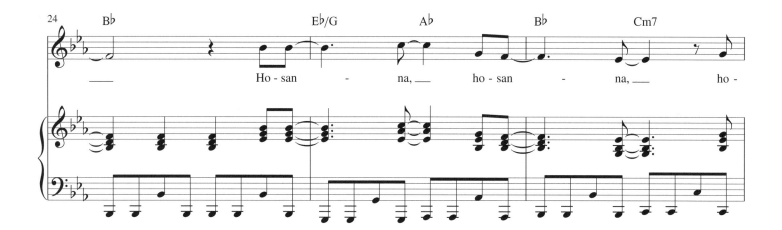

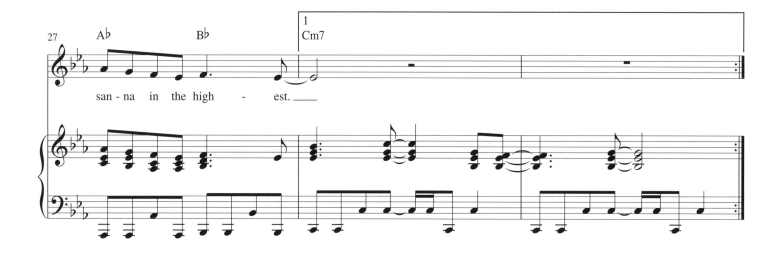

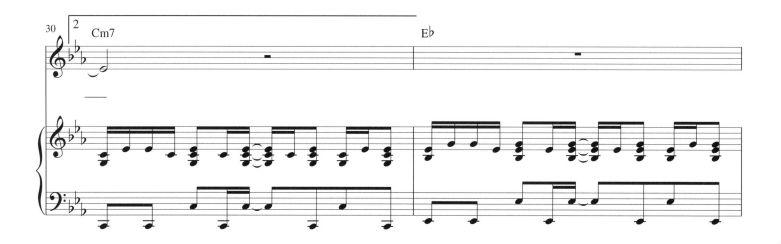

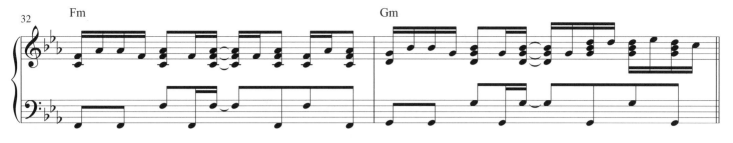

Heal my heart and make it ____ clean, ____
Break my heart for what breaks Yours, ____

o - pen up my eyes to the
ev - 'ry-thing I am for Your

things un - seen. ____
King - dom's ____ cause, ____

Show me how to love like ____ You ____ have loved me.
as I walk from earth in - to ____

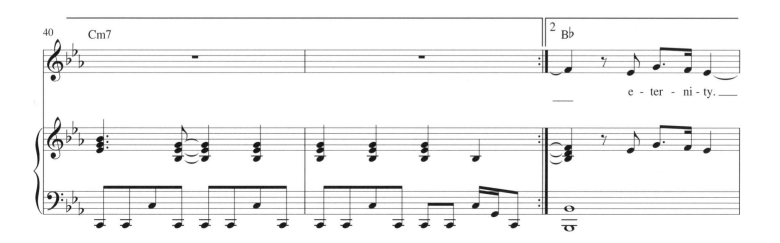

____ e - ter - ni - ty. ____

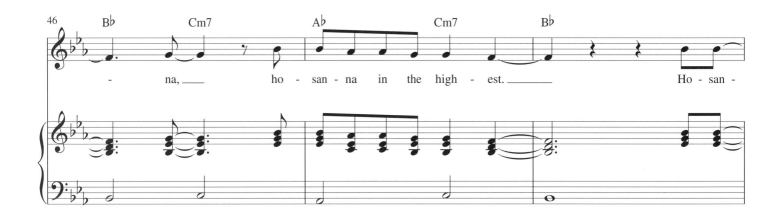

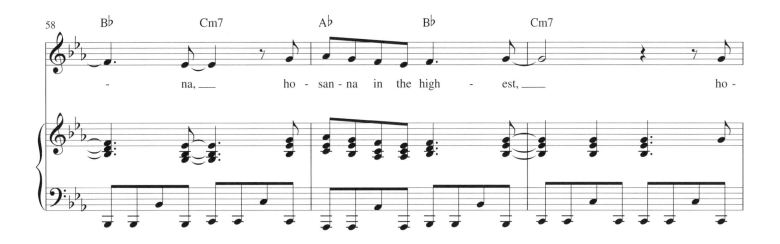

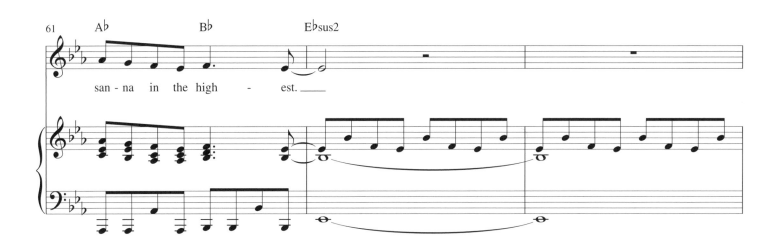

Jesus Messiah

Words and Music by CHRIS TOMLIN,
JESSE REEVES, DANIEL CARSON
and ED CASH

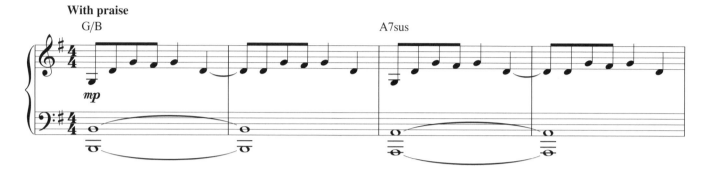

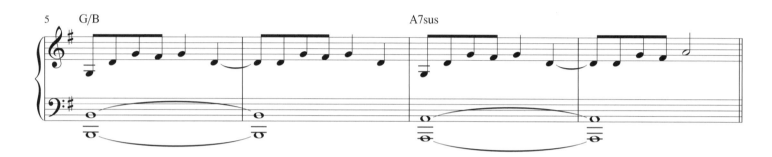

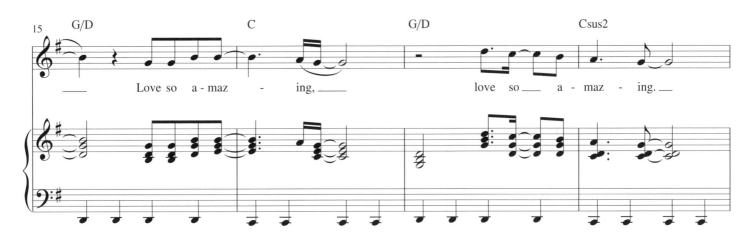

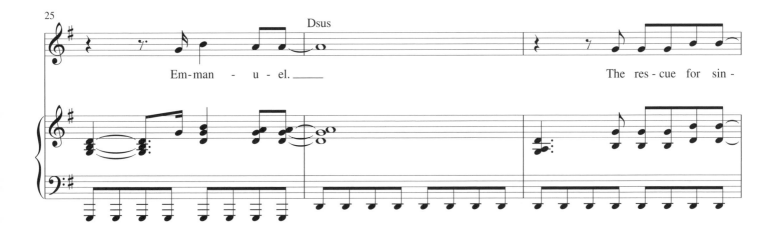

-ners, ____ the ran-som from heav - en. ____

To Coda ⊕

Je - sus Mes-si - ah, ____ Lord of all. ____

His bod - y the ___ bread, __ His blood the ___ wine, __

bro - ken and poured out, all for ___ love. __ The whole earth ___ trem - bled and the

veil was __ torn. _____ Love so a - maz - ing, ____

D.S. al Coda

love so __ a - maz - ing, __ yeah. __ Je - sus Mes - si -

CODA

All our hope _____ is in You, ___ all our hope __

_____ is in You. _____ All the glo - ry to You, __

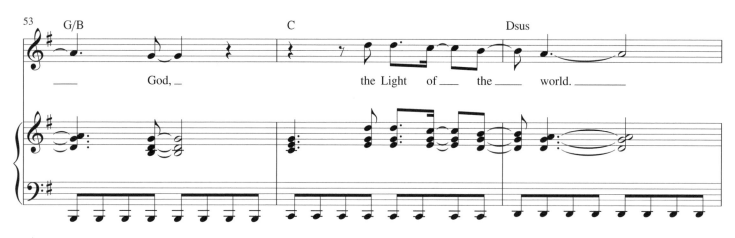

-en. ___ Je-sus Mes-si - ah, ___ Lord of all. ___

___ Je-sus Mes-si - ah, ___ Lord of all. ___

You're the Lord _ of all, ___

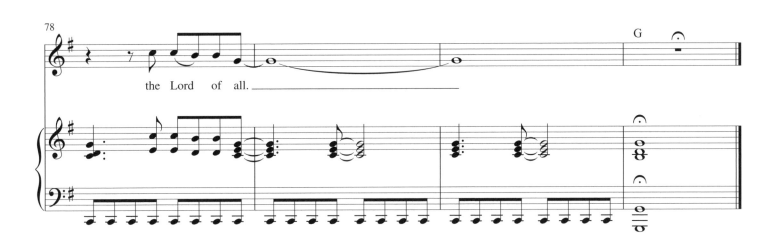

the Lord of all. _____

Mighty to Save

Words and Music by BEN FIELDING
and REUBEN MORGAN

Ev-'ry-one needs com-pas - sion, a love that's nev-er-fail-

-ing. Let mer - cy fall on ___ me. Ev-'ry-one needs for-give-

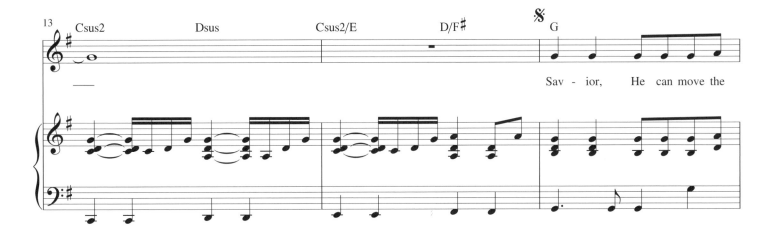

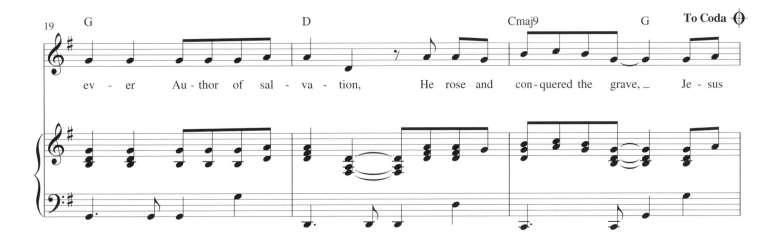

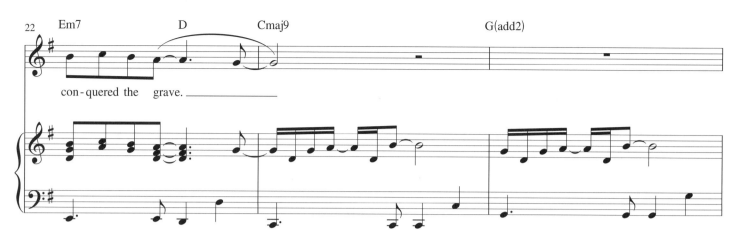

con-quered the grave. _____

So take me as You find _

_____ me, all my fears and fail - ures; fill my life a - gain. _

_____ I give my life to fol - low ev-'ry-thing I be-lieve _____ in. Now

D.S. al Coda

I sur - ren - der, _____ yes, I _____ sur-ren - der. _____

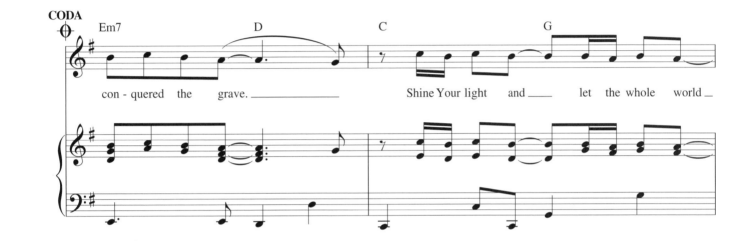

CODA

con - quered the grave. _____ Shine Your light and _____ let the whole world _____

_____ see we're sing-ing for the glo - ry _____ of the ris - en _____ King. _____ Je - sus,

shine Your light and _____ let the whole world _____ see we're sing - ing

for the glo - ry ___ of the ris - en ___ King. ___ Sav - ior, He can move the

moun - tains. My God is might - y to save, __ He is might - y to save. __ For -

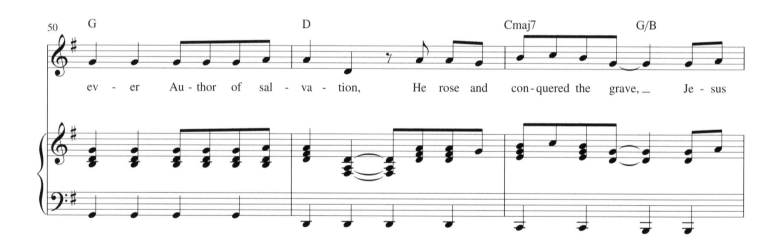

ev - er Au - thor of sal - va - tion, He rose and con - quered the grave, __ Je - sus

con - quered the grave. __ You're my Sav - ior, You can move the

moun - tains. God, You are might - y to save, __ You are might - y to save. __ For -

ev - er Au - thor of sal - va - tion, You rose and con - quered the grave, __ yes, You

con - quered the grave. __

You are might - y to save. __

Our God

Words and Music by JONAS MYRIN,
CHRIS TOMLIN, MATT REDMAN
and JESSE REEVES

With power

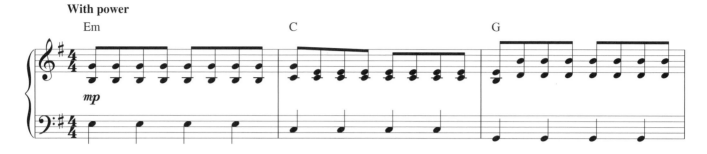

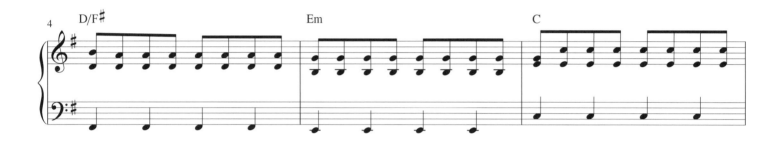

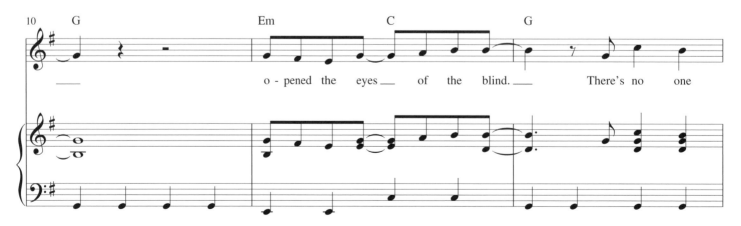

like You, _ none like _____ You. _____

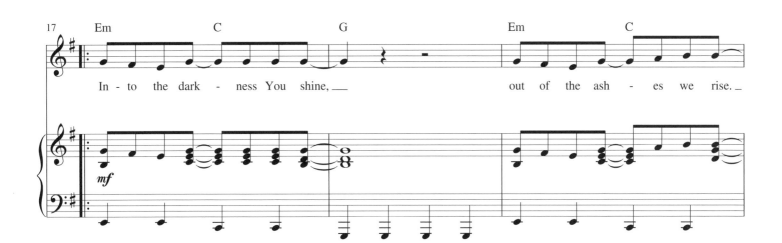

In - to the dark - ness You shine, ___ out of the ash - es we rise. _

_____ There's no one like You, _ none like _____

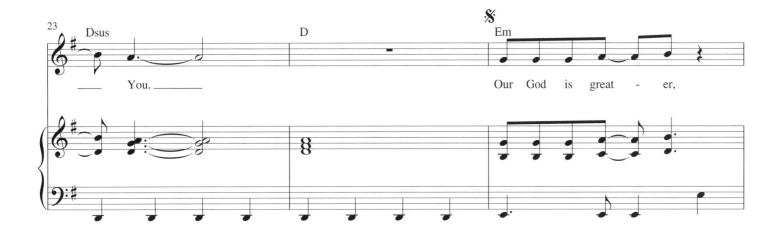

_____ You. _____ Our God is great - er,

our God is strong - er. God, You are high - er than an - y oth - er.

Our God is Heal - er, awe-some in pow - er, our God, our God.

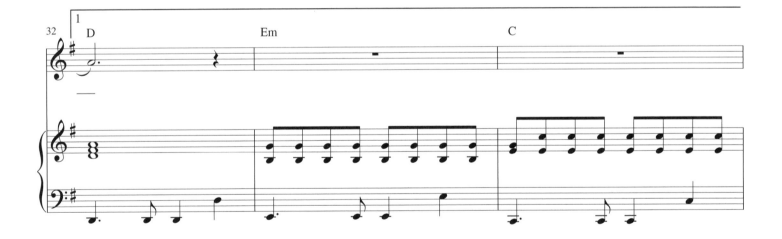

CODA

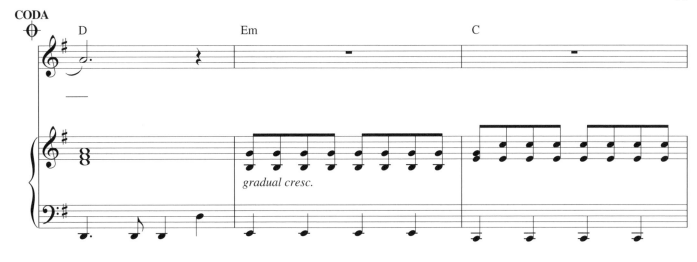

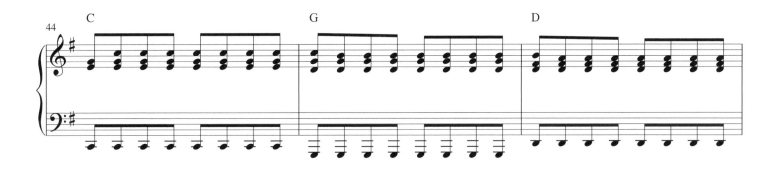

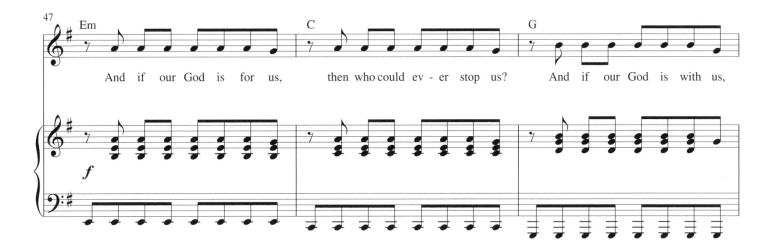

And if our God is for us, then who could ev - er stop us? And if our God is with us,

then what could stand a - gainst?__ And if our God is for us, then who could ev - er stop us?

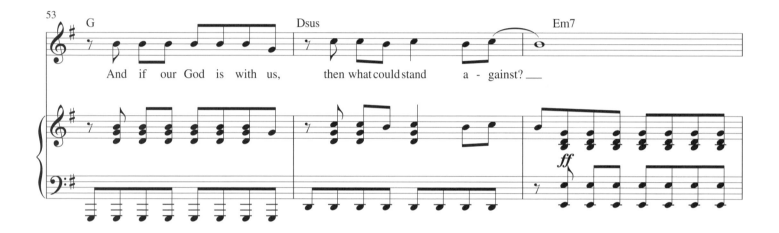

And if our God is with us, then what could stand a - gainst? __

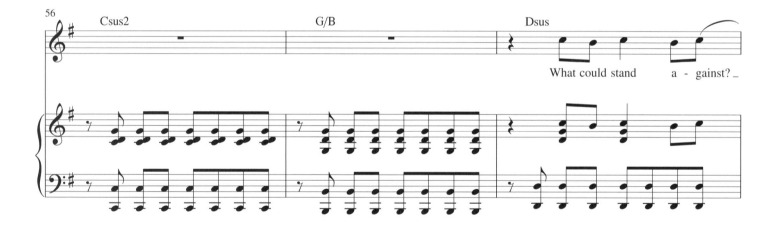

What could stand a - gainst? _

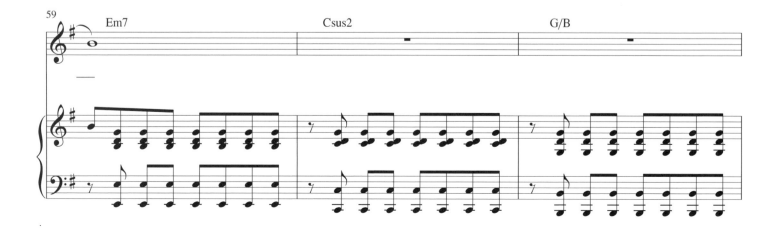

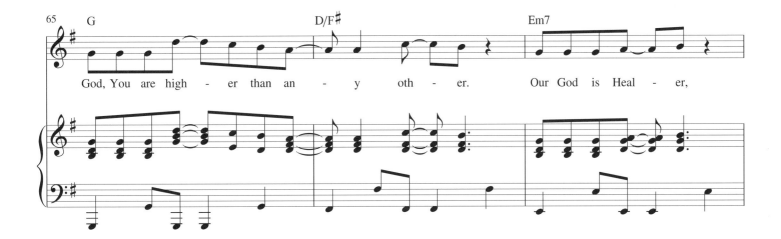

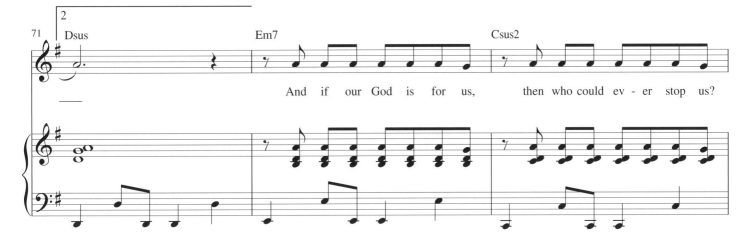

And if our God is with us, then what could stand a - gainst? _

_ And if our God is for us, then who could ev - er stop us? And if our God is with us,

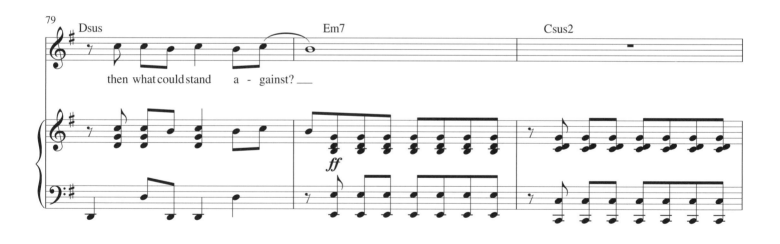

then what could stand a - gainst? ___

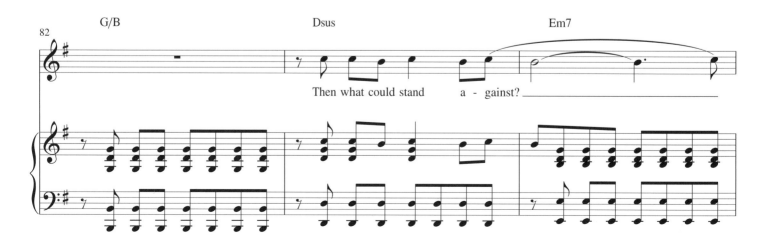

Then what could stand a - gainst? ___

Our God is great - er, our God is strong - er. God, You are high - er than an -

- y oth - er. Our God is Heal - er, awe-some in pow - er, our __ God, __

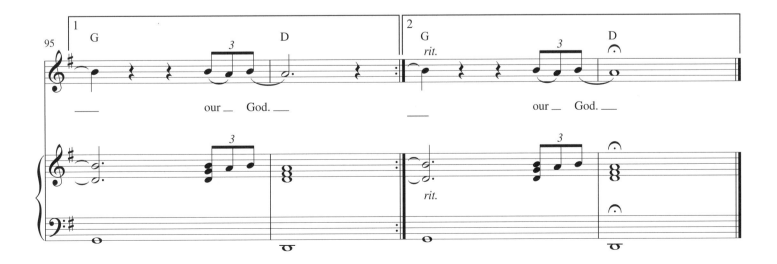

__ our __ God. __

our __ God. __

Revelation Song

Words and Music by
JENNIE LEE RIDDLE

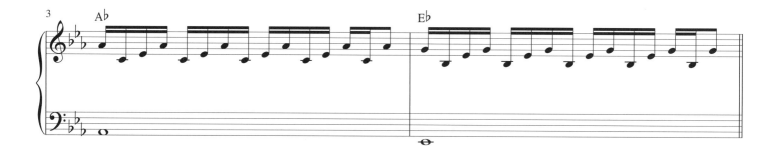

Wor-thy is the Lamb who was slain. Ho-ly, ho-ly is He.

Sing a new song to ___ Him who sits on

Heav-en's mer - cy seat. ___

Ho - ly, ho-ly, ho - ly is the ___ Lord God ___ Al-might - y,

who was ___ and is ___ and is ___ to come. ___

With all cre - a - tion, I ___ sing praise to the King of kings. ___

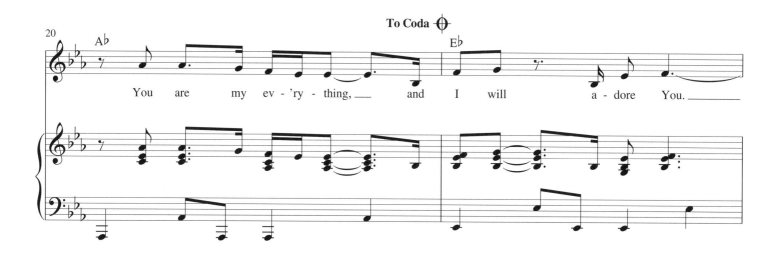

You are my ev - 'ry - thing, ___ and I will a - dore You. _____

___ Yeah, ___ I will a - dore You. ___

Clothed in rain - bows of ___ liv - ing col - or, ___

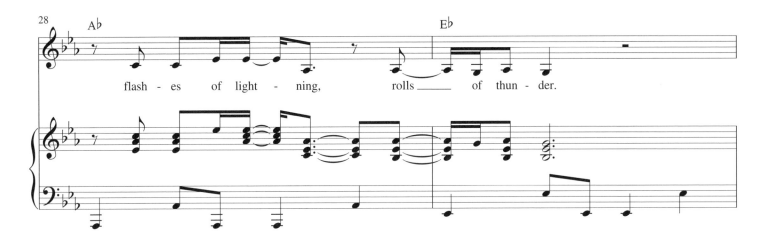

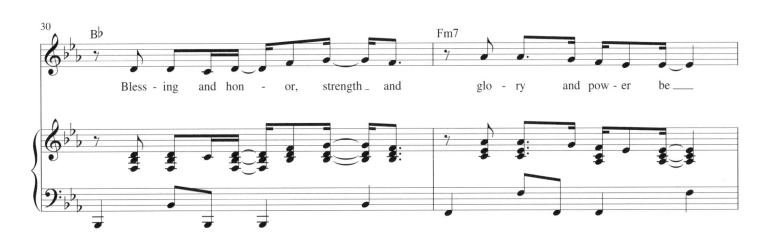

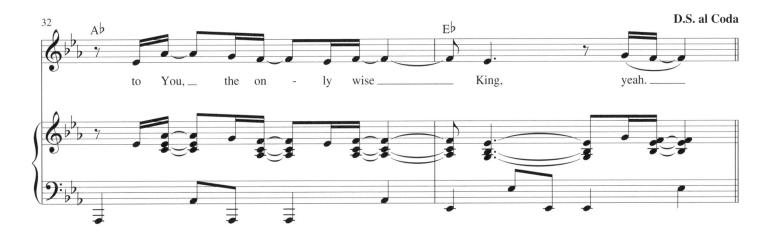

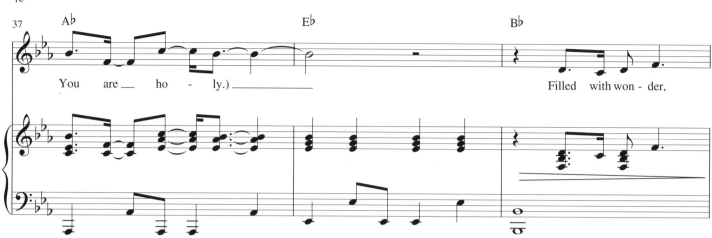

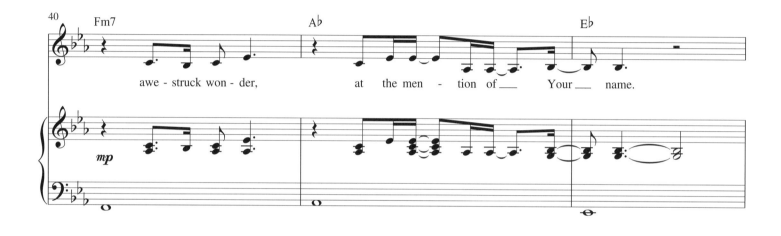

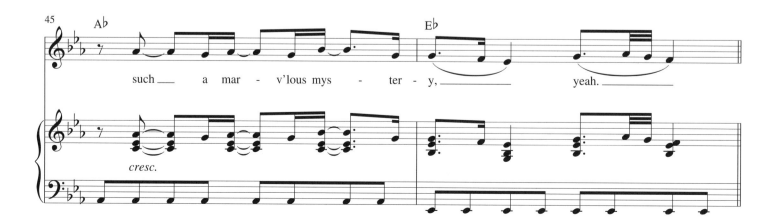

Ho - ly, ho - ly, ho - ly is the __ Lord God __ Al - might - y,

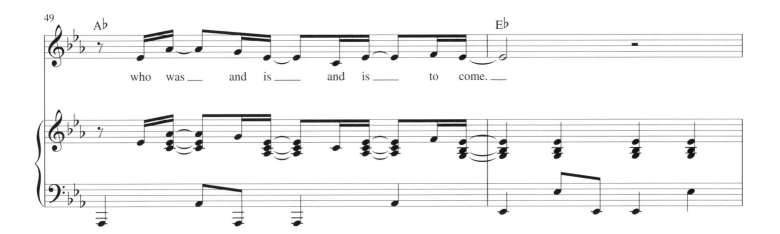

who was __ and is __ and is __ to come. __

With all cre - a - tion, I __ sing praise to the King of kings. __

You are my ev - 'ry - thing, __ and I will a - dore You.

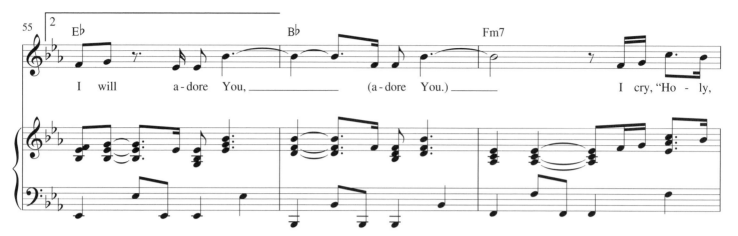

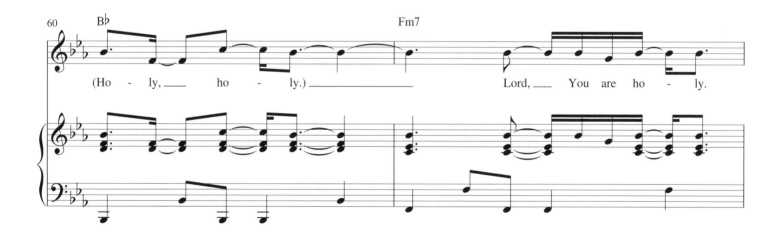

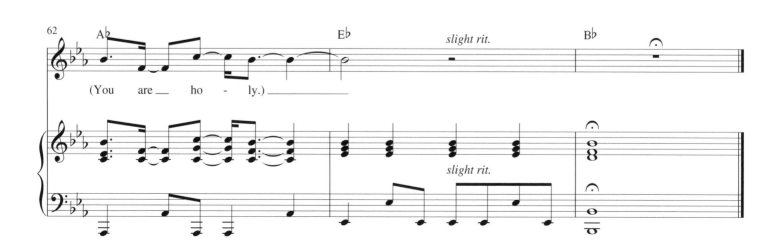

Stronger

Words and Music by BEN FIELDING
and REUBEN MORGAN

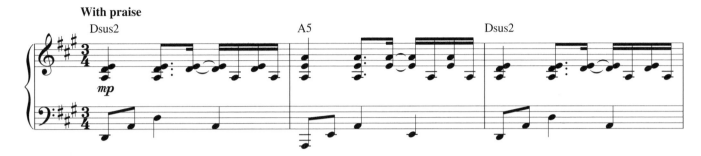

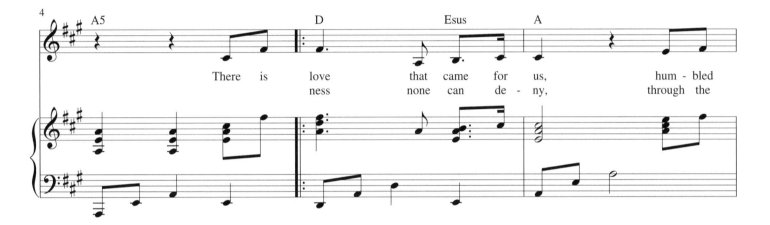

There is love that came for us, hum-bled
ness none can de-ny,

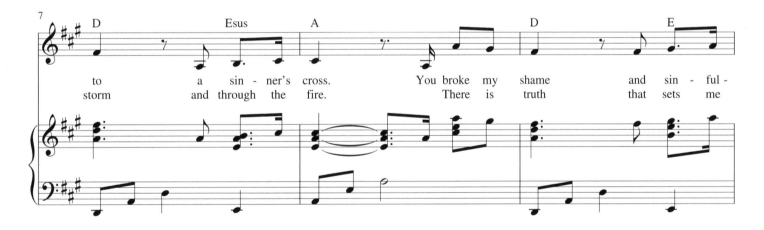

to a sin-ner's cross. You broke my shame and sin-ful-
storm and through the fire. There is truth that sets me

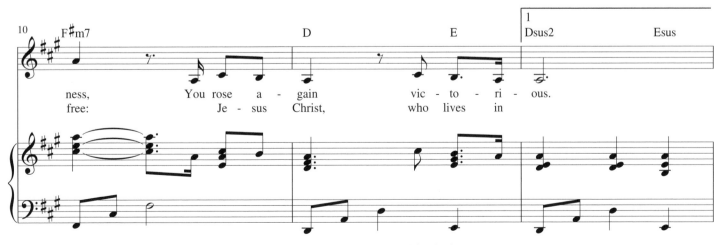

ness, You rose a-gain vic-to-ri-ous.
free: Je-sus Christ, who lives in

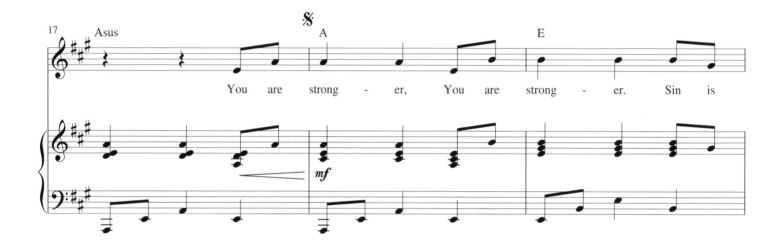

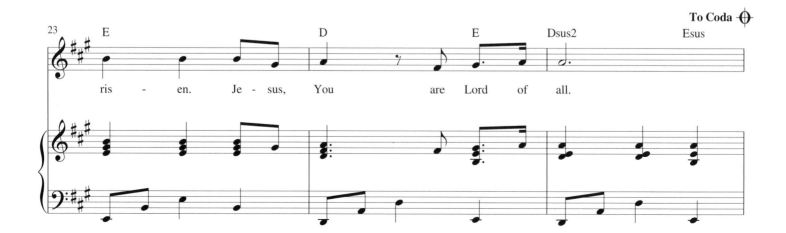

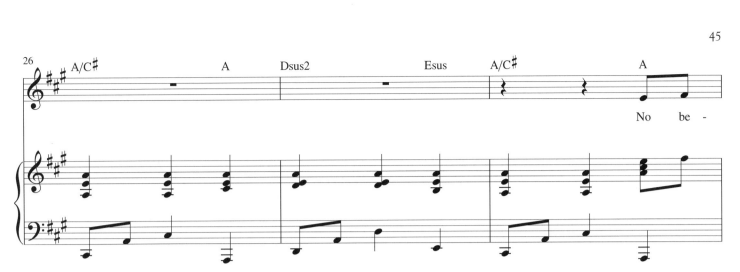

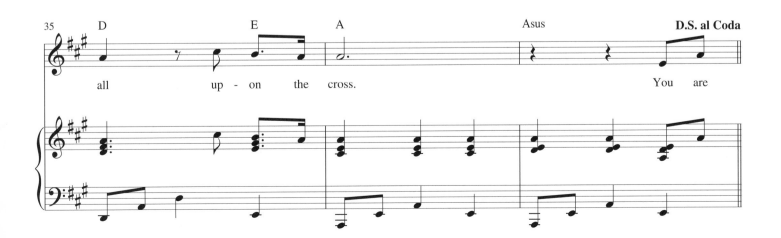

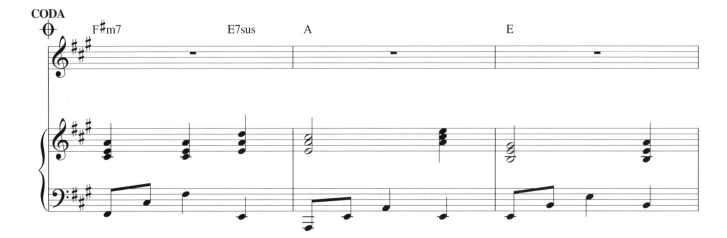

CODA

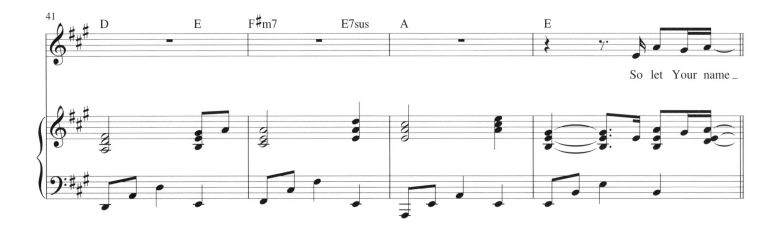

So let Your name _

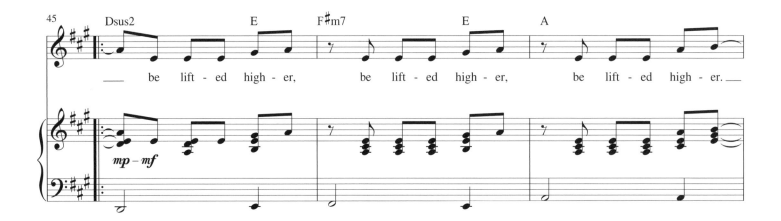

_ be lift - ed high - er, be lift - ed high - er, be lift - ed high - er. _

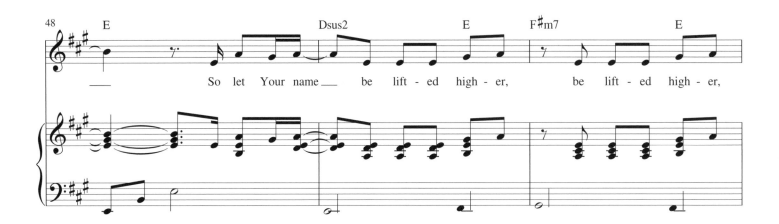

So let Your name _ be lift - ed high - er, be lift - ed high - er,

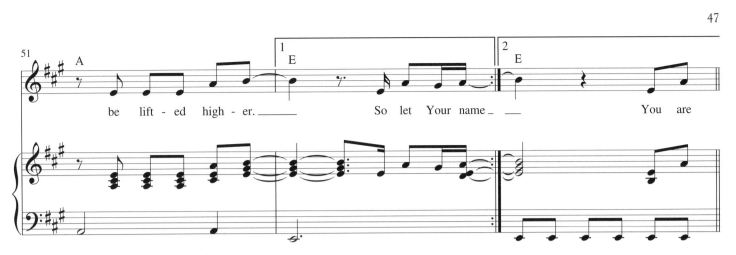

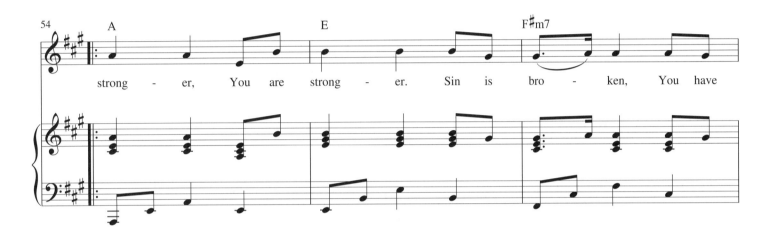

Your Name

Words and Music by PAUL BALOCHE
and GLENN PACKIAM

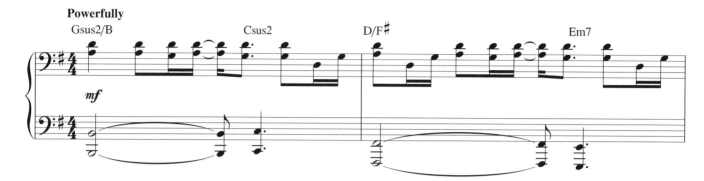

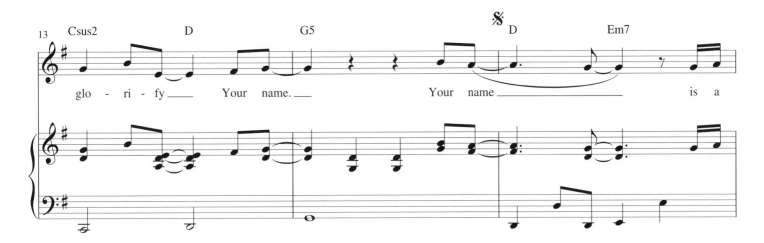

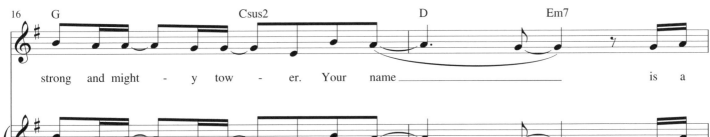

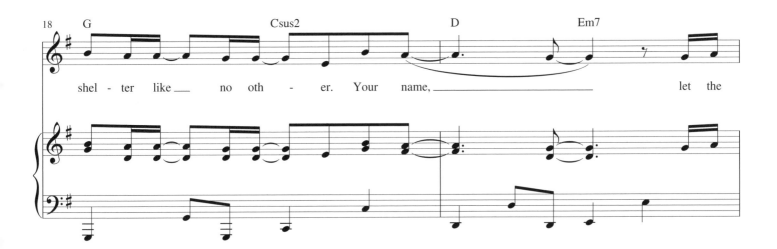

na - tions sing it loud - er, 'cause noth - ing has ___ the pow - er to save ___

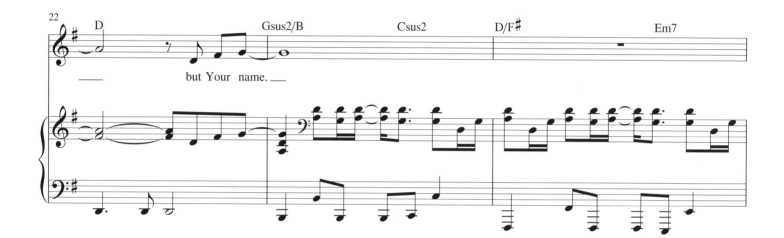

___ but Your name. ___

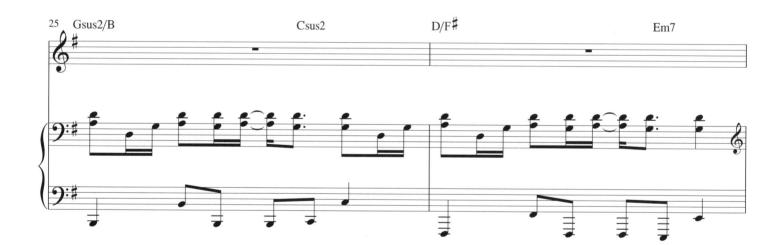

Je - sus, in Your name we pray, ___ come and fill our ___

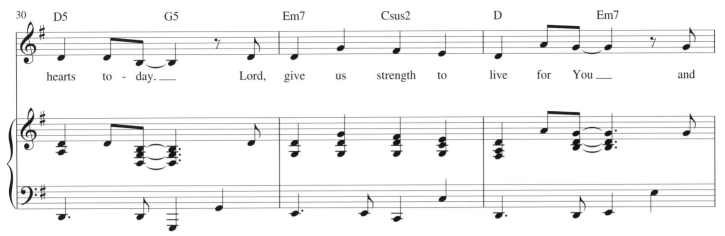

hearts to - day. ___ Lord, give us strength to live for You ___ and

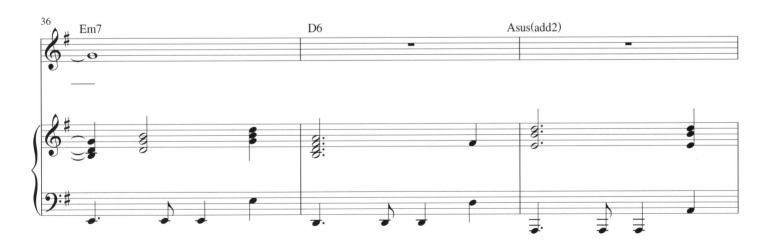

D.S. al Coda

CODA

glo - ri - fy ___ Your name. _____ Your name ___

but Your name. __

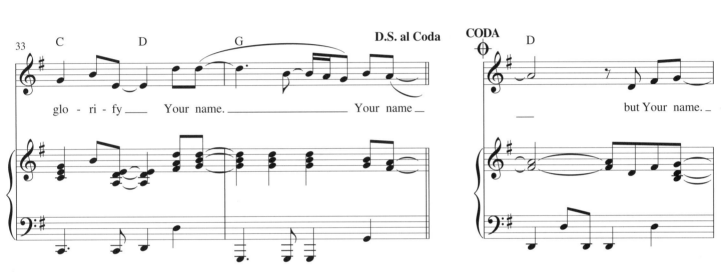

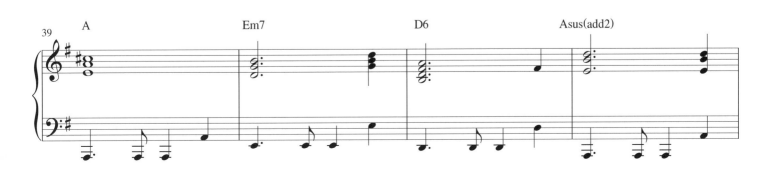

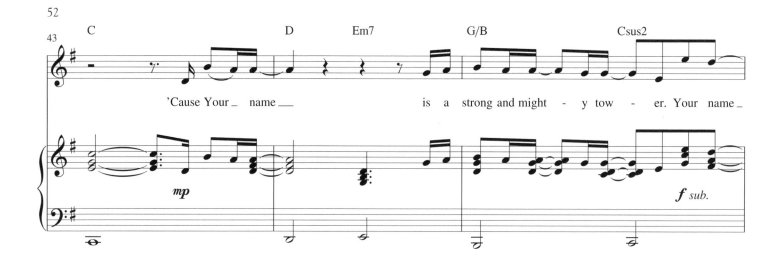

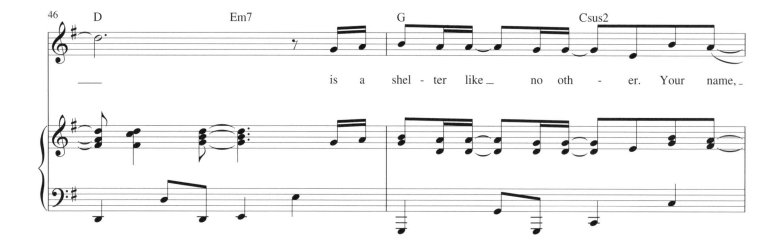

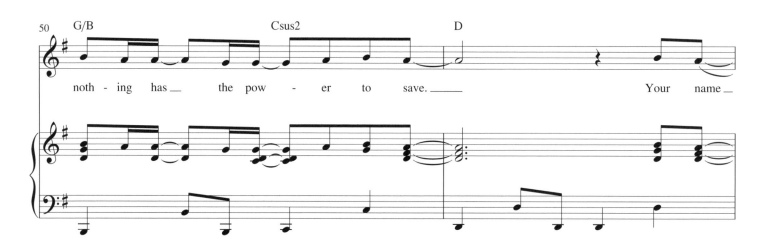

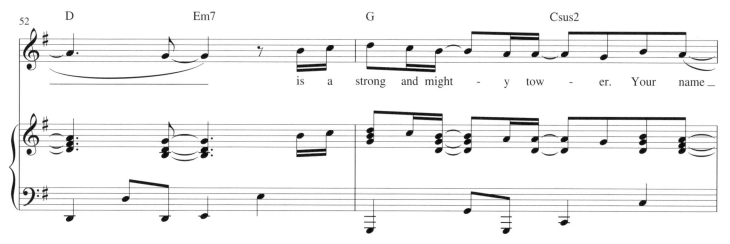

is a strong and might - y tow - er. Your name

is a shel - ter like ___ no oth - er. Your name, ___

let the na - tions sing ___ it loud - er, 'cause

noth - ing has ___ the pow - er to save ___ but Your name. ___

Na na na na na na.   Na na na na na na.

Na na na na na na.   Na na na na na na.

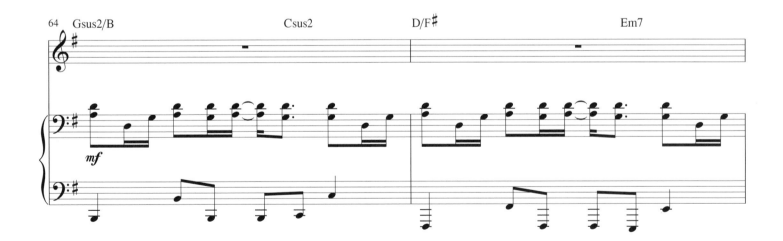

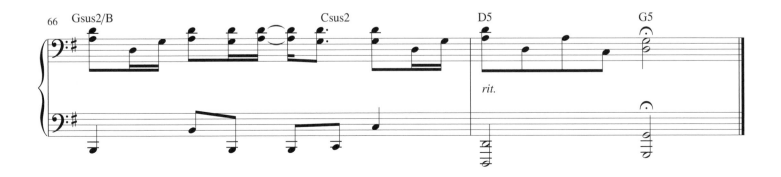

Whom Shall I Fear
(God of Angel Armies)

Words and Music by CHRIS TOMLIN,
ED CASH and SCOTT CASH

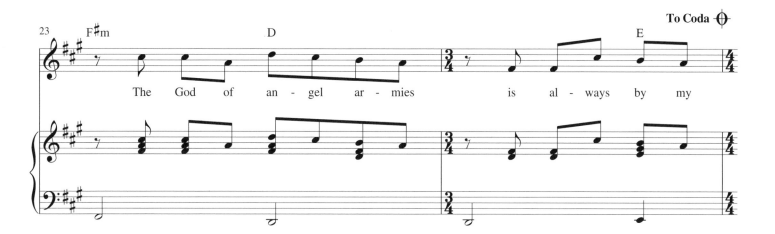

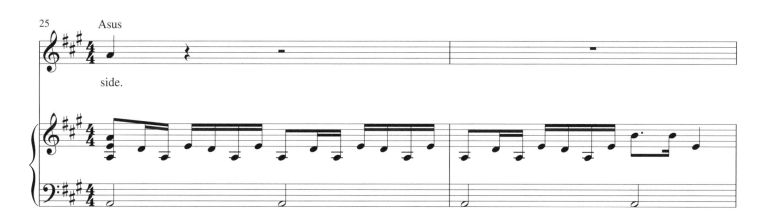

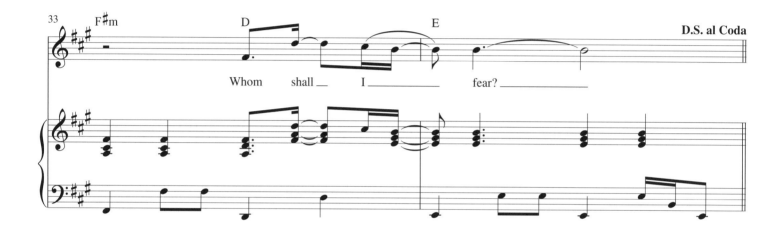

hands. _____ I'm hold - ing on ____ to Your

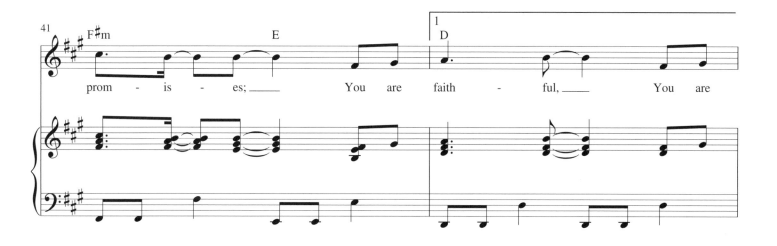

prom - is - es; ____ You are faith - ful, ____ You are

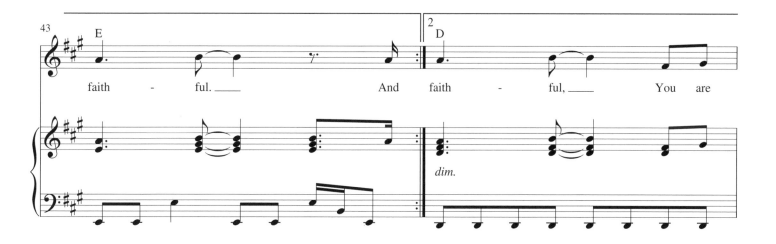

faith - ful. ____ And faith - ful, ____ You are

faith - ful, ____ You are faith - ful. _____

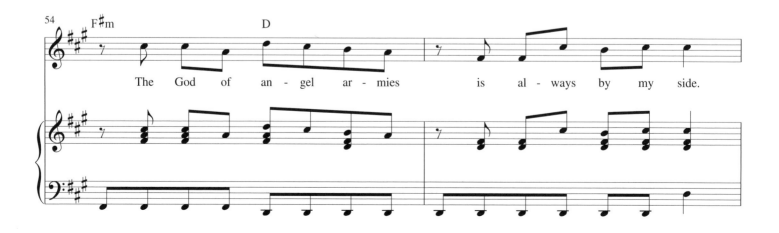

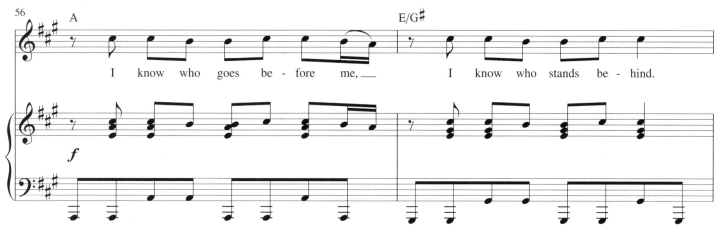

Your Grace is Enough

Words and Music by
MATT MAHER

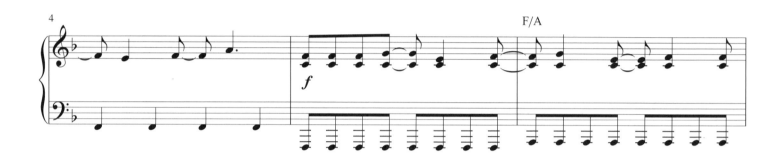

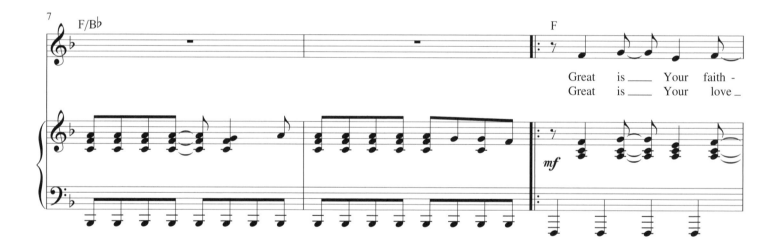

Great is ___ Your faith-
Great is ___ Your love ___

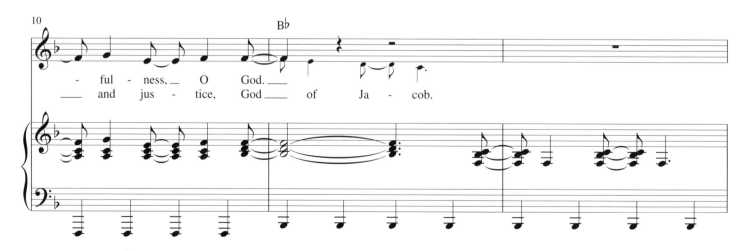

-ful - ness, ___ O God. ___
___ and jus - tice, God ___ of Ja - cob.

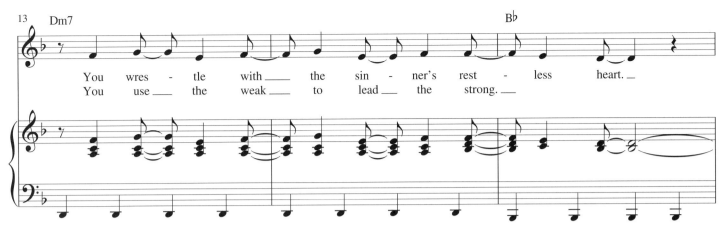

You wres - tle with ___ the sin - ner's rest - less heart. ___
You use ___ the weak ___ to lead ___ the strong. ___

You lead ___ us by ___ still wa - ters in -
You lead ___ us in ___ the song ___ of Your ___

- to mer - cy, ___ and noth - ing can ___
___ sal - va - tion, ___ and all ___ Your peo -

___ keep us ___ a - part. ___
- ple sing ___ a - long. ___

So re - mem - ber ___ Your

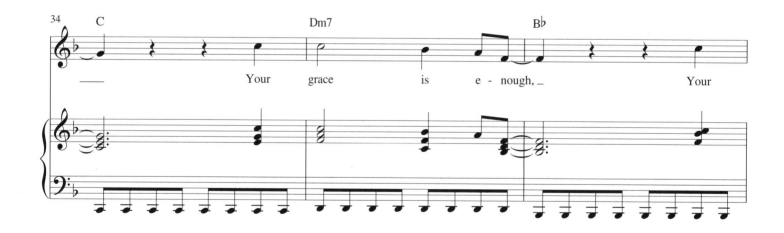

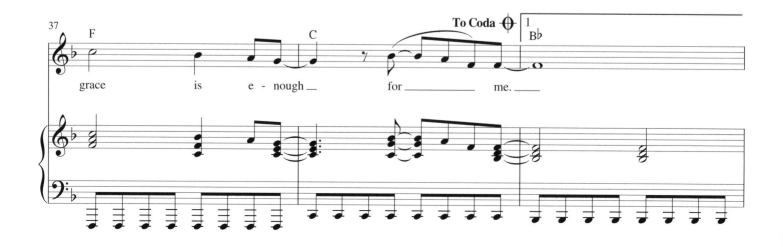

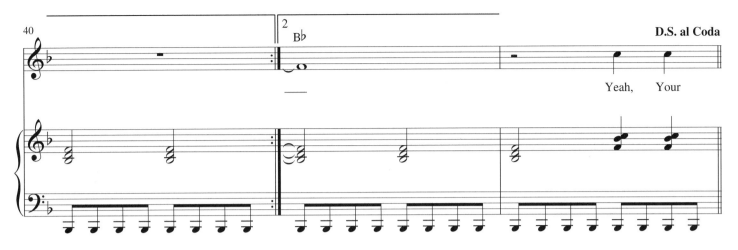

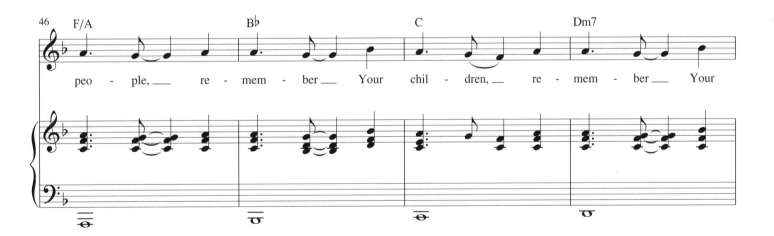

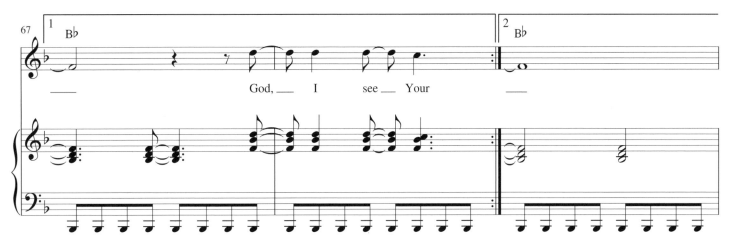

God, __ I see __ Your

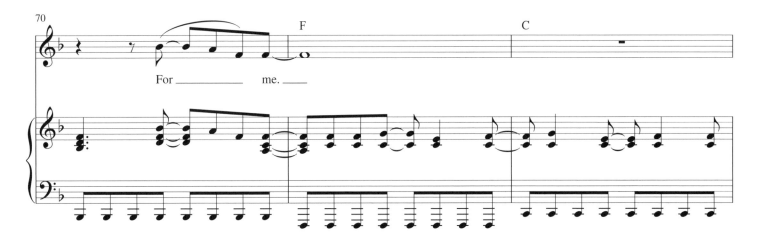

For _____ me. ____

It's e - nough __ for __ me. _____

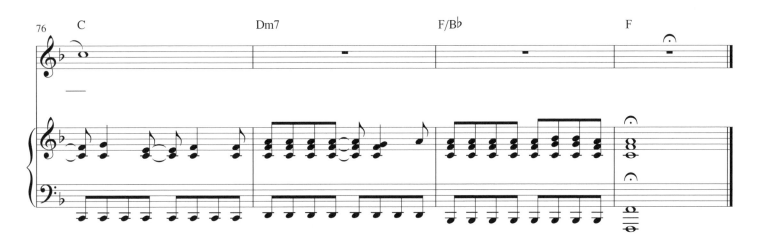